Plagiarisms

John Watson
Plagiarisms

Plagiarisms
ISBN 978 1 76109 074 5
Copyright © text John Watson 2021

First published 2014 by Picaro Press

This edition published 2021 by
Ginninderra Press
PO Box 3461 Port Adelaide 5015
www.ginninderrapress.com.au

Contents

Love at Donnafugata	7
Sylvie	18
The Fifth of October	55
La Forza del Destino	61
Lighea	70

Love at Donnafugata

Chapter 4 of *Il Gattopardo* by Giuseppe Tomasi di Lampedusa

Outside, a voice. Angelica appeared;
To give herself protection from the pouring rain
She'd gathered up in haste a peasant's cape,
A *scappolare*. In its dark, blue folds
Her body seemed more vulnerable and slight,
And under its wet hood her eyes gazed anxiously,
Their green bewildered and voluptuous.

This clash of beauty and rusticity
Lashed at Tancredi like a whip. He rose, and ran,
Without a word, to kiss her on the mouth;
The crowded room seemed far away; he felt
As if by kissing her he laid a claim
Once more to Sicily, the lovely, faithless land
The *Falconeri* held for centuries,

But which now passed to him
Its carnal pleasures and its fields of golden crops.
Angelica's return ensured delays
Before the family closed the house and left;
The weather too seemed much beguiled. The gale
Abated and a warm St Martin's summer held
Tancredi and Angelica in its arms.

That weather which is luminous and blue
And opens like a calm oasis in the harsh
Progression of Sicilian seasons, now
Inveigled, with its sweetnesses and warmth,
The entire palace; sensuality
At Donnafugata was the more seductive for
Its being so constrained by custom's weight.

Some eighty years before, these rooms had been
A meeting place for all that the eighteenth century,
Caught in its dying throes, had favoured; then
Indulgent pleasures, often quite bizarre,
Were witnessed by its vaulted walls. Since then
The Restoration, and the austere Regency,
Had put to flight its powdered cherubim.

Of course these wraiths had not entirely gone,
But hibernated under dust in attic rooms.
Angelica's arrival made them stir;
And when Tancredi saw her wet from rain
(He was already loud in love for her)
These entities revealed themselves like ants disturbed
By sunlight, swarming, indiscriminate.

Even the towers and domes themselves evoked,
In their rococo architecture – fluttering, flushed,
And multiple – the thought of flesh, its curves
And fields and landing stages, entrances
And bays, the burgeoning of flanks and breasts.
Then every opening door and billowing palisade
Seemed like a bed alcove in welcoming gauze.

Centre and motor of this awakening
Was the marriage of Tancredi and Angelica,
Certain, yet not immediate; and thus
This interval of sensual restraint
Made every visit by Angelica
A time of travelling in uncharted corridors,
Through rooms leading to rooms without an end.

Accompanied by her father or a maid,
Angelica was soon a frequent visitor;
Her father would return at once (to solve
Imaginary plots against him by his staff);
The maid would vanish to the servants' wing
To spend the time in gossiping or drinking coffee:
Tancredi and Angelica were alone.

He wanted to amaze Angelica
By touring the palace and its inextricable
Knot-garden of conservatories, state rooms,
Long galleries, chapels, theatres, saddling rooms,
Stairs, terraces and porticos – all vast
With fragrances persisting from a shadowed past –
And other even less frequented rooms.

These were the long-disused apartments, rooms
Which formed a deeper, still more redolent labyrinth,
And where their wanderings seemed interminable.
These rooms, unvisited and undisturbed,
Offered the lovers endless vistas – some
Which even Don Fabrizio had never seen
(A fact he thought the measure of a house).

The lovers now embarked for Cythera
On board a ship composed of draped and dappled rooms.
Within this labyrinth they soon cast off
Some easily distracted chaperone,
Cast off and set a course through tortuous
And winding passages where, compassless and tossed
By tumultuous seas, they sought their native shores.

They were alone, unwatched except by some
Long-faded portrait, eyes half blurred by its unknown
And inept painter – or some shepherdess,
Lost to her flocks in an apartment's gloom,
Who gazed down vaguely and consentingly,
From frescos crumbling into flesh-toned, clinging chalk.
They might as well have walked on Crusoe's beach.

Sometimes the governess could still be heard
Retreating, fading, down some distant corridor:
Angelicà, Tancrèdi, *où êtes-vous?*
Then silence would resume, to be disturbed
By scuffling rats in ceilings high above
Or rustlings from some long forgotten letter, blown
By a mysterious wind across the floor.

These rooms could be relied upon to yield
The pleasures of such startlement, excuses for
The reassuring touch of flesh on flesh;
And with them always, ever vigilant
And unforgetting, Eros led them on,
And drew them out of childhood into something more
Pervasive, darkly daring, filled with risk.

Not far from childhood, love delights to play
The game of being lost then found in faded rooms.
Here each would hide and tremble to be claimed
Behind some canopy or torn brocade;
Here hands seize hands prolonging like a gaze
That gesture dear to indecisive sensualists:
His urgent fingers pressed and parting hers.

Once, in the shadow of the painted scene,
Arturo Corbera at the Siege of Antioch
(Propped against a wall) she trembled, then
Unmasked, with cobwebs on her dusty hands,
She was embraced. At this, equivocally,
She cried, No, Tancredi! No! although her eyes like jade
Seemed even then to offer him the world.

One luminous, cold morning she arrived
And trembled strangely in a dress of summer voile.
Beside her, on a sofa's tattered silk,
He pressed her in his arms for warmth; her breath
Disturbed his hair. The shadows turned away,
So painful and ecstatic seemed desire, restrained
In one long prolongation of delight.

The rooms in these abandoned palace wings
Had neither plan nor name. And like those travellers
On New World terraces, pristine and strange,
They named the rooms they crossed for their return:
A bedroom with an ostrich feather bed
They called 'the feather room', a crumbling set of stairs
'The staircase of the earth' and, often lost,

They turned through half-remembered corridors,
Their puzzled wonderment excuse enough once more
For murmuring contact. Often they would lean
From paneless windows into some small court
To get a glimpse of gardens and thus tell
Which wing they had traversed, which way they must take back.
But sometimes they were comprehensively lost.

And sometimes willingly lost, they'd lean and gaze
From windows into unfamiliar courtyards, blank,
Anonymous, unused – repositories
For some odd detritus or stray cat's corpse,
Or food flung from some window; then, at times,
They'd find their gaze met by some ancient former maid
Who stared out blankly from another wing.

One afternoon they found in gauzy light
An old carillon in its dusty box which still
Surprised them with its charming melody,
To whose sweet disillusioned gaiety
They rhymed their kisses, only noticing
The notes had ceased for some long, ebbing interval
While they still kissed to ghostly memories.

The carillon in its narrow wooden box,
Its copper cylinder traversed by little tongues
Of raised steel, and its halting melody,
'The Carnival of Venice', echoing.
While such surprises stood like tragic reefs
Through all these sailing days, one dark and sultry day
They found surprises of a different kind.

A narrow hall divulged a room in which
A wardrobe hid a door; the centuries-old lock
Soon gave to fingers pleasantly entwined,
And soon a narrow marble staircase led
By rose-pink steps towards a padded door,
Its tapestry in threads. This door led to a room,
A room which for a moment puzzled them.

The rose-pink staircase opened on a room
Whose coloured stucco ceilings bore unusual
And, luckily indecipherable, reliefs;
Damp had obscured them and had charred the glass
In mirrors hung too low along the walls;
The fireplace bore intaglio whose naked forms
Were mutilated by a hammer's blows.

The damp had stained the walls with sombre shapes.
Disturbed, Tancredi did not want Angelica
To wander in this room. A bureau held
A bundle of small whips, some wrapped in silk,
Some silver-handled. Locking this at once,
Tancredi said, 'Let's go, my dear, there's nothing here.'
His kisses seemed still distant, lost in thought.

Tancredi was disturbed, preoccupied;
They pulled the wardrobe back against the door, and left
And all that day his kisses were remote
Dream-like as if in expiation, grave…
But later, in another suite of rooms
Tancredi kissed Angelica with such dark force
She cried aloud, and found her mouth was bruised.

Each day they ventured on a floating past,
Discovering in some rooms a hell redeemed by love,
In others, paradise by love profaned.
The separation of these two grew blurred;
Each day the urge to end their timeless game,
And take the prize, became – for each of them – acute,
The corridors led only to themselves.

They visited remote domains from which
No echoing cry might ever reach the outside world.
Absorbed, intent and lacking gaiety,
They sought that yielding cry; most dangerous
Were those still fragrant rooms in certain wings,
Where rolled-up mattresses could be spread at a touch
And nothing dimmed the rhetoric in their blood.

One day Tancredi, mindless, reasoning
With all the singular logic of the tides, resolved
To put an end to their protracted flight,
Cast anchor in the tropics of these seas
Which tossed them daily. Soon he was convinced
That, under garland-trailing Cupids, Angelica
Already seemed to wade on such a shore.

Already she had murmured as she leaned
Half fainting at a counterpane unfolded, mute,
Complicit, 'I am yours'; the male overwhelmed
The man, the girl seemed woman in that light
Already. Then they heard the church bell ring
Almost above their heads. They checked themselves. They smiled,
And knew that soon Tancredi had to leave.

Tancredi and Angelica would find
That these had been the happiest days of both their lives;
Of that they were, of course, still unaware.
When they were old and uselessly made wise,
Their thoughts would turn to this desire, boundless
Because restrained, with countless proffered beds declined,
Desire sublimed a moment into love.

Those days had been a preparation for
A marriage which, erotically and otherwise,
Was no success; yet radiant in themselves,
These days were exquisite, like melodies
Which will outlast their long forgotten works
And hint at, in their delicate, veiled gaiety,
The opera which will use them without skill.

Sylvie

From the short novel by Gérard de Nerval

I. Indulgent Nights

I left the theatre where I sat each night
    Indifferent both to stage and house
Until the opening of the second scene;
    Then emptiness was filled at once;
        Her incandescent radiance
        Brought all these tableaux back to life.
I lived in her appearance on the stage
And thought that she declaimed for me alone.

Her smile filled me with infinite delight.
    Her voice was resonant as dusk
And, when the lights were dimmed, her face was wreathed
    In gold poured from the chandelier
        (In which that small world seemed to float)
        And in this glow, against the dark,
She was like one of those divine Hours, carved
In high relief at Herculaneum.

These were strange times, like eras which succeed
    A revolution or collapse
Of Empire: thus we were familiar
    With contraries brought into flux,
    With indolence, activity,
    Renewal, weariness, and vague
Utopias, sputtering zeal, akin
To the wayward times of Apuleius. Thus,

We looked for new birth from the rose bouquets
        Isis herself might bring…
And when at night the young goddess appeared,
        We felt shame at our wasted days…

Ambition had retreated, leaving us
        On shores of lethargy;
Our only refuge from the multitude
        Was to climb the poet's Ivory Tower…

Upon those heights we breathed at last an air
        Of solitude. We seized the cup
Of legend and, intoxicated, drank
        To poetry and spectral love!
        Vague figures, shades of mist and rose,
        Replaced real women at such heights:
It was our habit to regard them all
As Goddesses who were as remote as wraiths.

My uncle, who had lived much of his life
        In the century before our own,
Had warned that actresses were women born
        Without a heart; as evidence,
        He showed me portraits, locks of hair,
        And faded letters which he said
Were perfumed tokens of betrayal… Thus
I fell into the habit of mistrust.

I left the theatre, dark once more, subdued;
        And visited a club nearby,
Where melancholy yielded to the noise
        Of sophistry. A young man spoke:
        'I've seen you often at the play,
        The same play watched repeatedly.
For whom do you go?' I named the goddess. 'Ah!'
He pointed out a young man playing whist:

'He is her latest lover.' But I smiled:
        'Someone, somewhere, must play that rôle.
As for myself, each night I seek and find
        A likeness, nothing more.'

I went out through the reading room. I glanced
        At the latest paper, curious
To note the market's flux. A Ministry
        Had fallen; I was rich again…
        I turned the page and read these lines:
        Fête du Bouquet Provincial:
Tomorrow the Senlis archers will present
The Bouquet to Loisy. These simple words

Revived in me a flush of memories
        Of the provinces: the horn and drum
Still echoing in the forest; garlands held
        By village girls at such a fête;
        A heavy wagon drawn by oxen
        Passed to receive their gifts, and we,
The children of the country, took our part
In rituals which would outlast monarchies.

II. Adrienne

I went to bed, but found no rest, and as
        I lay in a kind of waking sleep,
My childhood thronged about me. In this state,
        When dreams still wait their rising moon,
        A lifetime's memories are compressed:
        A château with its pointed roofs
Built in the time of Henry IV, enclosed
By elms and lindens, shimmered in my mind.

Girls danced in rings and sang old melodies
        Learnt from their mothers, in a voice
And accent so entirely pure, one seemed
        To be in the Valois, where the heart
        Of France beat for a thousand years.
        I was the only boy who danced.
Sylvie had come with me, a country girl
Vibrant and fresh, her eyes as black as night.

And, until then, I loved no one but her.
        But now I saw a light-haired girl
Dancing alone. She was called Adrienne
        And, by the dances' ancient rules,
        We who were caught within the ring
        Were asked to kiss. The music rose;
I pressed her hand. We kissed. I felt her hair
In ringlets on my cheeks. Unease seized me.

The rules also decreed that she must sing;
        We sat in the circle. She began,
In a delicately modulated voice,
        A ballad, full of passionate tears,
        About a princess in a tower,
        Imprisoned there for having loved.
Each stanza ended with a quivering trill
More thrilling from the throat of one so pale.

Twilight descended from the massive trees
        Around us; a silver vapour spread.
The quivering song had ended. With its trill
        We thought ourselves in Paradise.
        A mist had found us on the lawn,
        And moonlight shone on her alone.
I ran to where some ribboned laurels stood,
And placed a shining wreath on Adrienne's head.

They said that she had royal Valois blood.
        She'd been allowed to join
Our rustic games, but must soon disappear
        To go back to her convent school.

Sylvie was crying afterwards. I found
        The reason lay in Adrienne's crown.
I said I'd bring another, but she said
        She was unworthy. Tears prevailed…
        In Paris I could not resolve
        These two affections: Sylvie's warm
And tender friendship; and the strange demands
Of an impossible love enveloping me…

A year had passed, and Adrienne became
        An even more remote mirage:
I heard that at her family's decree
        She'd taken convent vows.

III. Resolution

These half-dreamed memories made me see that this
        Unreasonable, unreasoning love,
The cloak I cast beneath an actress's feet,
        Had in reality begun
        With Adrienne, flower of night
        Unfolding to a rustic moon –
Pale Adrienne who had become a nun…
Were nun and actress one upon the stage?

And why had I forgotten for so long
        Poor Sylvie whom I loved so well?
I see her window framed by vines, the bird
        Loud in his cage below the sill.
        She spins and sings. The spindle whirrs.
        Perhaps she's waiting for me still.
The lavish legacy my uncle left
Might have been saved with Sylvie at my side.

And as I thought of Sylvie, so the thought
        Of travelling to see her grew.
Where might she be? Of course! The Festival
        Of the Bow was on this very night,
           And she who loved to dance would dance
           All night. If I could reach her there,
These three years of neglect and negligence
Might vanish like a dream, in her dark eyes.

What time was it? I had no watch. The clock
        In my extravagant rooms had stopped:
Its gilded dome on which stood Time himself,
        Its tortoiseshell, its caryatids,
        Diana leaning on her stag
        In bas-relief, were dumb
To tell the hour, or whether I could leave
And reach the dance at Senlis by the dawn.

I went downstairs. The porter's clock struck one.
        And in the Place du Palais-Royal
A group of cabs stood waiting in the street.
        The driver had to ask the way.
        'Near Senlis, twenty miles or less'…
        How bare is the Flanders road at night
Until it meets the woods. Then double rows
Of trees, like embracing figures, stand in mist.

Ploughed land and meadows, dreary market towns,
        Give way at last to villages
Where apple blossom frosts the dark like stars.
And while my carriage slowly climbs the hill
        I think of fragrant days:

IV. A Voyage to Cythera

Some years had passed since I saw Adrienne
        Before the château. Loisy now
Was glowing for its patron saint's name day.
        At once amongst the Archer Knights
        I took my place. The festival
        United Compiègne, Senlis
And Chantilly. This rustic cavalcade
Began with mass for the contesting teams.

A long walk through the town and villages
        Led to the embarcation for
The banquet on an island in a lake
        Fed by the Nonette and the Thève,
        And shaded by a linden grove
        With poplars interspersed in rows.
A ruined temple was the banqueting hall,
And floral barges took us to its banks.

It may be that the crossing of this lake
        Had been devised deliberately
To conjure up the Watteau Cythera.
        And certainly we felt transformed,
        Despite our modern costumes, by
        Such an Arcadia. I sat
With Sylvie and her brother, who complained
Of my neglect of them. Then Sylvie said:

'We're only villagers and Paris is
        Above us. He's forgotten me.'
I wanted to restrain her with a kiss
        But she was distant, offering me
        Her cheek half-heartedly.
        And still my admiration grew;
She was no longer just the village girl
Whom I had scorned for fair-haired Adrienne.

The banquet ended in a planned surprise:
        A wild swan was released from flowers
Beneath which it had been confined. It soared,
        While wreaths and garlands on its wings
        Fell back to earth; and, if he could,
        Each boy seized one to press upon
His partner's brow. Here I was fortunate,
And Sylvie smiled this time at my embrace.

V. The Village

I left them at the guardhouse at Loisy
        And, entering the little wood
Which joins the forest of Ermenonville,
        Expected every path to lead
        To the convent walls. At times the moon
        Was hidden by dark cloud, and then
Amongst Druidic boulders I could feel
The ghosts of Armen slain by Romans here.

The lakes were mirrors in the plain. Which one
        Had been our host? The air
Was warm, the heather comforting. I slept,
        And then went on at first light.

When I awoke, I saw the convent walls
        And, further on, Thiers Abbey, high
Above the trees, with crumbling arch and naves,
        Pierced by trefoils; and, in the sun,
        The moated walls of Pontarmé;
        While further south the glittering turrets
Of La Tournelle; and past there, on the slopes
Of Montméliant, the towers of Bertrand-Fosse.

My thoughts were captives of the previous day.
        I thought only of Sylvie. Yet
The convent walls and bell were eloquent
        Suggesting Adrienne within.
        I thought the highest rock might look
        Into the grounds Yet, with the sun,
This seemed a profanation and the idea
Dissolved in thoughts of Sylvie's upturned face.

'Why not awaken her myself?' I said,
        And set off through the fragrant woods;
Some spinners, their hair in crimson handkerchiefs
        Already were at work. I passed,
        And knocked at Sylvie's door.
        She looked up from her lace and smiled.
I told her of my wanderings in the woods
And Sylvie said, 'I hope you're not too tired –

Because I want you to accompany me
        To Othys, to see my great-aunt there.'
I'd scarcely answered when she leapt up, bent
        To arrange her hair before a mirror,
Put on a rough straw hat, and turned;
And we were following the Thève
Through meadows filled with buttercups, then on
Into the dapple of Saint-Laurent woods.

Blackbirds were singing, hidden in the trees.
        And periwinkles at our feet
Recalled Rousseau, who treasured these blue flowers
        On sprays of doubled leaves. Sylvie
        Was more concerned a single flower
        Should not be crushed beneath our feet,
Than for that sage's *La Nouvelle Héloise,*
From which I quoted passages by heart.

Sylvie was picking strawberries. She said,
        'And is this book of Rousseau's good?'
I said, 'It is sublime.' 'Better,' she asked,
        Than August Lafontaine?'

'It has more tenderness,' I said. 'Well then,
        I'll ask my brother, when he goes
To Senlis next, to buy it for me.' And
        She picked more strawberries.

VI. Othys

Emerging from the woods, we came upon
        A clump of purple foxgloves. 'Look!'
Cried Sylvie, 'We must pick them for my aunt.
        She loves to have them in her room.'
        And soon, across a level field
        We saw a village steeple. Next
We heard the pleasant rustling of the Thève,
Lithe in its bed of flint and sandstone – here,

Quite narrow and determined, near its source,
        A tiny welling lake, enclosed
By gladioli and dark irises
        And meadow flats. One narrow field
        Was farmed by Sylvie's aunt and, since
        Her husband's death, managed for her
By villagers. Her cottage door stood open;
And Sylvie called, 'Good morning, aunt. We're here –

Your children, who have walked for miles – and are
        Most dreadfully hungry.' Sylvie placed
The foxgloves in her arms and tenderly
        Embraced her. Only then she thought
        To introduce me… 'He is my sweetheart.'
        Then I too kissed her and she said,
'A fine young fellow, and with fair hair too!'
Sylvie laughed. 'Yes, he has got nice soft hair.'
'How well your dark hair goes with his, my dear.'
        And Sylvie smiled again. 'We must
Give him some breakfast, aunt.' She brought brown bread
        And milk and sugar from a cupboard,
        Placing these on painted plates,
        With bowls of strawberries in milk,
And cherries from the garden. Next she placed
A vase of flowers on the tablecloth.

Her aunt objected: 'This is mere dessert.
        You must let me do something now,'
And threw sticks on the fire for the pan.
        'You mustn't touch this with your hands
        Which make such lace as cannot be
        Excelled, even in Chantilly.'
'Then, aunt – let me look upstairs in your room
For old lace I might copy. Where's the key?"

Her aunt laughed; 'Nonsense! Nothing's locked. Go up.'
        But Sylvie cried, 'One drawer
Is always locked,' and seized a little key,
        And ran triumphantly upstairs.

I followed. There above the wooden bed,
        With beams of sunlight striking it,
A young man, black-eyed and with rosy lips,
        Stared from a gilded frame.

Some naïve artist at the royal hunt
        Had captured with simplicity
This uniformed young gamekeeper; near it,
        A similar portrait of his wife,
        Lissom, capricious and serene
        In her embroidered smock. She holds
A pet bird in her hand... This was, I saw,
The very person downstairs at the hearth.

I cried out, 'Oh, how pretty she was then!'
        And Sylvie laughed. 'She was like me,'
Then opened with her key the famous drawer.
        She drew from it a faded dress
        Of taffeta. Shaking it out
        She said, 'I'll try it on and see
How well it suits me.' She unhooked her dress,
Its printed cotton fell around her feet.

The rustling taffeta was made for her;
        Her slim waist matched it perfectly.
'These wide sleeves! Aren't they quaint?' she cried.
        But from their hoop-shaped slits,

Her bare arms were revealed; her slender throat
        Rose with a startled grace
From ribbons interlaced through faded tulle,
        Like Greuze's *Village Bride*.

'You must have powder,' I exclaimed. She began
        To rummage in the drawer again.
What treasures it contained! What tinsel, colours!
        An amber necklace, Chinese paste,
        Mother-of-pearl…and from this trove
        Silk stockings with embroidered clocks
And a pair of buckled slippers of white silk.
She sighed, 'I must wear these.' But suddenly

Her aunt's voice and our breakfast summoned us.
        Sylvie commanded, 'Go on down.'
Reluctantly I left and went downstairs
        To bacon rashers in the pan
        Until again at Sylvie's call
        I climbed the wooden steps. 'Be quick,'
She murmured, pointing to the wedding suit
Laid out for me. She waited on the stairs.

I dressed and we descended hand in hand
        To the astonished gaze, and tears,
And startled cry of, 'Oh, my children!' First
        She wept, then smiled through burning tears.
        It was a vision of her youth
        At once delightful and yet cruel.
We sat down gravely at her side but soon
Our gaiety returned. Then she began

To speak of wedding days and happiness
        And amorous songs which had been sung
Around her bridal table – echoing still –
        And leaning on her husband's arm
        To walk back from the wedding dance,
        The sound of flutes above the applause…
We lingered in this glow; Sylvie and I
Were wife and husband all that summer day.

VII. Chaâlis

Four in the morning. Soon the carriage will
        Reach La Chapelle. Nearby, a road
Where Sylvie's brother took me once; I think
            It was on Saint Bartholomew's Day…
            His pony flew, and drew our cart
            On unfrequented woodland roads
As if a witch's Sabbath summoned us,
Until we reached the Abbey at Chaâlis…

Again the carriage floats on memories:
        Chaâlis! This keep of emperors
Is now in ruins: cloisters frame the lakes
            Which Charlemagne ruled. But mists
            Have not dissolved the allegories
            Painted in pink on chapel vaults…
With Sylvie's brother I observed, that night,
What must have been a costumed mystery play…

The actors, dressed in hyacinth and gold
        And azure, in the opening scene
Discoursed with angels on the end of time;
            They sang of transience; then, one rose
            And holding high the Flaming Sword
            Bade them applaud Christ Glorious.
This luminosity was Adrienne,
Transfigured – as she was by her vocation –

And haloed by her pasteboard cloud. Her voice
        Had gained in strength and range; she sang
In the Italian style with bird-like trills.
        I thought of Loisy, and the ring
        Of dancers. And yet these memories,
        Dislodging as the carriage swayed,
Perhaps were dreams… And Sylvie's brother was
A little drunk that night. For we had stopped

And gone into the guard-house where the swan
        With outspread wings affected me;
Inside were trophies – bows and arrows– and
        A tall grandfather's clock, a dwarf
        Cut from sheet iron… Yet I'm sure it was
        The guard who led us to the play…
These reveries receded like a dream
As I left the coach – a short walk from Loisy.

VIII. The Loisy Dance

I reached the Loisy dance just at that stage
        Of pleasing melancholy when
The lights grow dim at the approach of dawn.
        The lindens' lower branches sank
        In darkness as their tops turned blue
        In the advancing light. The flute
Failed in its contest with the nightingale.
I scarcely knew this pale dishevelled crowd.

But there was Lise, one of Sylvie's friends.
          She kissed me, saying, 'Well! It's our
Long-lost Parisian stranger! So, you've come.'
          'Just now, by post coach. Where is Sylvie?
          Has she gone?' 'I thought you'd know.
          She never leaves the dance until
The morning light… She simply loves to dance…'
Then I saw Sylvie turn, and gaze at me.

A youth had joined her for the last quadrille
          But, seeing me, bowed and withdrew.
Daylight was flooding as we left. Some flowers
          Drooped in the coils of Sylvie's hair,
          And bouquet petals at her waist
          Were scattered on her crumpled dress.
We walked along the path beside the Thève.
'Sylvie,' I said, 'You do not love me now.'

'Dear friend,' she sighed, 'you must be reasonable.
          Things don't fall out as we would wish;
You spoke to me of *La Nouvelle Héloïse,*
          And I have read its fateful words,
          The girl who reads these words is lost…
          Remember how, at my aunt's, we dressed
As bride and groom? If only you'd stayed here!
I often thought of you in Italy –

You must have seen girls prettier than me
                In Italy.' 'But no!' I cried,
'None with your features, none as beautiful.
                You seem to me to be some nymph
                From Legend. And our country is
                As beautiful as Italy.'
'But what of Paris?' As I shook my head,
I thought I saw that fair, elusive Shade…

'Sylvie!' I cried and knelt down at her feet.
                In tears I told her of my fickle
Indecision, and of the sombre wraith
                Which haunted me. 'Sylvie,' I said,
                'You must save me. For you alone
                Have always been the one I loved.'
She turned with tenderness, about to speak,
When others joined us on the river path.

At first we saw just Sylvie's brother, who
                Was laughing at some joke and who
Took rather much refreshment at the dance;
                Sylvie's admirer then appeared
                With awkward deference. I thought
                Him not too serious a rival.
'We must go home,' said Sylvie, offering me
Her cheek, which did not trouble her admirer.

IX. Ermenonville

I had no need of sleep, so went again,
        Already saddened by the thought,
To see my uncle's house at Montagny.
            The key was kept now at the farm,
              But the yellow boards, the shutter's green –
              All seemed, as always, quite unchanged…
I stood amongst the polished furniture
And looked at some engravings for Emile.

The farmer said, 'The parrot's still alive.
        I've got him at my house.'
I looked across the garden, massed with weeds;
           One patch had been mine as a child.

Emotion now began to overwhelm
        My scattering of impressions. Here
The study held its books, old friends of one
           Whose memory they evoked. And there,
           Ranged on his desk, the Roman shards,
           Whole vases and medallions
He'd dug up in his garden. Gravely I said,
'I'd like to see the parrot,' and we left.

Entering the farm we heard the creature speak,
        Demanding lunch as stridently
As he had always done. He turned to stare
        Fixedly at me.

With gloomy thoughts I left the farmer's house,
        Longing for Sylvie. She was alive!
And not the sifting dust of memory
        Like all else here. And she alone
        Could still persuade me to return
        To country lanes where childhood sleeps…
With Sylvie in my thoughts I left the farm
And followed her as if she walked ahead.

I set out on the Loisy road, then thought
        Of walking through the woods
To Ermenonville. The interlace of trees
        Was scarcely parted by the sun.

Among the oaks were birches, quivering
        With tassels. Noon was hidden. Birds
Were silent. In that drift of leaves, I heard
        The green woodpecker's hollow tap.
        The signposts were illegible –
        I very nearly lost my way
But finally, with the Désert on my left,
I found the old men's bench and dancing-green.

A little further on, the lake shone through
        The branches as the sun had done;
And, at a turn, hazels and willows seemed
        At once familiar.

For it was here my uncle brought me, here
        To the Temple of Philosophy,
Unfinished and in ruins now, inscribed
        With resonant names: *Descartes, Montaigne,*
        In plaques which ended with *Rousseau…*
        The temple crumbles with the days
And Nature carelessly reclaims the ground
Which Art once briefly sought to take from her.

The roses too are gone. The raspberry
        And dog briar cover them.
But Vergil's privet flowers, as if to prove
        His words inscribed above the door,
        Rerum cognoscere causas.

I turned and saw the island's poplar grove
        And, in its shadows, Rousseau's tomb
From which his ashes vanished long ago.
        Rousseau! We have forgotten all
        You taught our fathers, all those faint
        Echoes of ancient wisdom. Still
We must take courage and, as you did at
The moment of your death, turn to the sun.

I saw the château with its rock cascade;
        The causeway with its four dovecots
Linking the two sides of the village; the lawn,
        The artificial lake –

All these receded in the constant hum
        Of insects. Yet the place repels
By artifice – and I retreat across
        The sandy heath with its pink heather.
        How lonely all these places seem
        With Sylvie gone from them. How fresh
The cascade seemed, seen through her eyes.
With what delight she hid amongst the rocks;

We went once to get milk. The dairyman
        Called out, 'How pretty is
Your sweetheart, fortunate Parisian!'
        This was the time she danced with me alone
        At the Festival of the Bow.

X. Curly-head

At Loisy everyone was up. Sylvie
        Seemed now to have a lady's air
In manner and in clothes. Her smile was still
        As charming, but more serious.
        We went upstairs. Her bedroom now
        Had changed. The warbling bird had gone;
The antique pier-glass and the flowered chintz
Were gone. Little of the past remained.

I said, 'Will you be making lace today?'
    'Oh, no. I don't make lace these days.
There's no demand – even in Chantilly.'
        'What do you do then?' She produced
        An instrument that looked like pliers:
        'Everyone makes gloves just now.'
I wanted us to leave. I looked towards
The Othys road, but Sylvie shook her head.

When had her aunt died? 'Let us go,' I said,
    'To Chaâlis.' She called a small boy
Who brought a saddled donkey. We set out.
        Somehow I could not bring myself
        To speak of what I felt. Instead
        I found myself describing life
In Paris, or discoursing on my travels.
She said, 'It must be sad so far away.'

'To see you makes me think so too,' I said.
    She sighed. 'These things are lightly said.'
And still I spoke of things irrelevant
        And half forgotten. She recalled
        Our catching crayfish at the bridge
        And then said, 'Do you remember when
You fell into the stream? Your foster-brother
Had to pull you out. Do you remember?'

'Oh, you mean Curly-head. And it was he
        Who told me I could wade across!'
I hurried on to change the subject, change
        From clouding memories when in fact
        I wanted only to be part
        Of Sylvie-in-the-present… I thought
Of Othys and the wedding clothes we wore,
And wondered what became of them. She frowned:

'Dear aunt!' she said, now weeping bitterly.
        'She lent the clothes to me
For the Carnival at Dammartin. She died
        Last year.' She looked away, in tears.

XI. The Return

Emerging from the wood we found ourselves
        Amongst the lakes at Chaâlis.
The tower of Henry IV and Gabrielle
        Glowed red against the forest's green.
        'A scene from Walter Scott,' she said.
        I smiled and took her hand. 'Sylvie!
You have been reading since I saw you last.
But, as for me, I'd like to give up books –

And visit places which survive the past
        And yet are filled with it:
The abbey where we played at hide-and-seek,
        And where you used to sing old songs.'

I wanted to hear Sylvie sing the song
        About the maiden carried off
While walking by her father's white rose garden.
        'No one now sings that song,' she said,
        'And I prefer the opera.'
        She sang an air… But I complained:
'I love those melodies which you've renounced,
And fear that you'll forget them all too soon.'

But something in her manner seemed remote;
        What could I say to her
Accompanied by a donkey and a boy
        Who never left us for a second?

And worse, I blundered into telling her
        About the unforgettable
Appearance of the ice-pale Adrienne
        Here at Chaâlis long ago.
        We even found the very room
        Where I had heard her sing. 'Sylvie!
If only I could hear your voice beneath
These very arches – then perhaps I might –

Just might – be free of this recurring dream
        Which still torments me like a wraith…'
But when I spoke the words of one such song
        She called it gloomy, and she seemed
        Distracted still. She took my arm.
        I sought the words eluding me
But in the water meadows where our path
Crossed interlacing streams, we fell silent.

Instead I found my thoughts had floated back
>   To Paris and the theatre lights.
Tonight what new role might Aurelia play
>   (For that was the actress's name)? Perhaps
>   The new play's Princess… And if so,
>   What pathos in the final act,
What passion in the love scene in the first!
But Sylvie sighed: 'You seem so far away,'

And in her softest voice began to sing,
>   *At Dammartin are three fair maids…*
'You see!' I cried, 'This isn't fair. You do
>   Remember those songs after all.'
>   'If you were ever here,' she said,
>   'I could remember many more.
But you must live in Paris, and I work here…
And I begin at sunrise: we should go back.'

XII. Père Dodu

I should have offered her my uncle's house,
>   Which I could still have bought (the estate
Was still intact, despite its several heirs),
>   I should have spoken, should have knelt,
>   But we had reached Loisy too soon,
>   And onion soup announced itself,
And, indoors, supper was delayed for us.
There in the gloom I recognised at once

The woodsman, Père Dodu, who in his time
>Had been a fisherman,
A poacher, shepherd, storyteller – and
>Who now made cuckoo clocks.

He also showed Ermenonville to the English,
>And took them to those places where
Rousseau had sat in thought; here (he would point)
>Were spent the philosopher's last days.
>Here, as a boy, Père Dodu had
>Helped tend the old philosopher's plants.
And it was he who squeezed the hemlock juice
Which Rousseau took unfailingly in coffee.

It had been said Père Dodu cured sick cows
>By saying the Scriptures back to front
While making with his foot the sign of the cross;
>But these days he disowned such things,

Declaring conversations with Jean-Jacques
>Had made him give up superstition.
'You've come to steal our girls, Parisian?'
>'I, Père Dodu?' 'Yes. Taking them
>Into the woods when the wolf's not there.'
>'But, Père Dodu, you are the wolf.'
'I was, as long as there were any sheep,
But now it's goats, and they can defend themselves.

But all you Paris folk are dangerous.
        Jean-Jacques was right. Man is
Corrupted by the poisonous city air.'
        'But aren't all men corrupt?'

At this the old man sang a drinking-song
        Which he persisted in, despite
Our outcry at a certain questionable verse.
        Sylvie would not sing… I found
        Her young admirer from the dance
        Oddly familiar. He rose.
'You don't remember me, Parisian.'
Someone beside me whispered in my ear:

'Your foster-brother! Surely you recall –'
        'Oh, it's Curly-head, of course!' I cried,
'You pulled me from the water, long ago.'
        And Sylvie laughed with Curly-head.

Then Sylvie, saying she was sleepy, stood
        And, going upstairs to her room,
Seemed to have quite forgotten me until
        She said, 'Tomorrow – visit us.'
        I sat with Père Dodu; he drank
        And mused. He said that Curly-head
Would be a pastry-cook and have a shop
In Dammartin, with Sylvie as his wife.

XIII. Aurelia

The morning coach to Paris seemed to wind
        Through forests which it could not leave.
Five hours to Paris! Yet the hours passed.
        I only needed to be back
            By eight – at which I took once more
            My usual seat. The play began;
This would-be Schiller seemed to have in mind
Aurelia's powers, for in the garden scene,

She was astonishing. When, in Act IV,
        She played no part, I went outside
To Madame Prevost's and bought a large bouquet
        In which I wrote affectionately,
            Signing myself *Un Inconnu,*
            And pledging future loyalties.
The following day I went to Germany
To bring some order to my drifting thoughts –

Perhaps to write the story of a man
        Who loves two women, and who was
Perpetually divided… Could this succeed?
        Sylvie was gone from me, and yet
            A single day sufficed to fuel
            My love for her. Her placid smile
Caused me to hesitate before the abyss
Of offering myself to Aurelia,

As one more in that motley company
>   Like moths in the consuming flame.
And then one day I read that she was ill.
>   I wrote at once; but Salzburg – and
>   Its mountains – may have introduced
>   A note of German mysticism…
She could not answer, for I still remained –
And put my faith in Chance and – *l'Inconnu.*

Months passed while I composed a theatre-piece
>   About Colonna and his love
For Laura who was, by her family,
>   Placed in a convent. He remained
>   As faithful to her memory
>   As to his mural art… There was
In this sad subject something much akin
To my own sorrows… Yet I longed for France,

And soon returned. And then I passed into
>   That Purgatory we call the Theatre.
Labouring in its wings I was its slave
>   In making something permanent
>   Of vague ideals… Aurelia
>   Agreed to play the leading role
In my German play. The day I read to her
Was memorable; I read with passionate zeal,

Since she had inspired the love scene in my play.
        I felt that she must recognise
My passion as I read… Then I disclosed
        The identity of *l'Inconnu.*
            She called me mad… She laughed, and yet
            Agreed that I might visit her…
She said, 'I'm waiting still to find the man
Who understands and loves me truthfully.'

I wrote to her again – effusively –
        But her replies were always kept
Within the bounds of friendship. Then, one day,
        She seemed more generous, and spoke
        Of one attachment she could not,
        Without great difficulty, break
'And if you loved me for myself,' she said,
'You'd want me to be yours and yours alone.'

But barely two months later I received
        A warmer letter; and at once
I hurried to her. On the way, I met
        A friend, who told me this: he'd heard
        A young man I had seen with her
        Had joined the cavalry in Algiers…
Next summer, at the races at Chantilly,
Aurelia and her company performed.

And there I met the manager – who had been
        The actor in Aurelia's play
The night I came from Sylvie and Loisy.
        I saw his qualities at once
        And asked him to perform for us
        In Senlis and in Dammartin.
The following day, while theatres were arranged,
I hired horses and, with Aurelia,

Rode to the Château of Queen Blanche for lunch.
        Dressed elegantly, with her hair
Outstreaming in the wind, Aurelia
        Seemed like a queen of former days.
        And afterwards we visited
        The château near Orry, where first
I gazed on Adrienne. Aurelia
Seemed strangely cool. And so I felt compelled

To tell her of that vision – Adrienne
        In moonlight and a gauze of mist –
And how that love had now been realised
        In her, Aurelia, luminous
        Onstage beneath the chandelier.
        She listened gravely. Then she said,
'You don't love me at all. I'm not that nun…
You crave a drama, not real flesh and blood.'

Aurelia said, 'I've lost all faith in you.'
          And, with these words, a flash of truth
Began to trouble me. This passion, born
          And nurtured, carried for so long…
          Perhaps this was not love, perhaps
          I had not found love… At Senlis
Aurelia pointed to the manager:
'Now there is the man who loves me truthfully.'

XIV. Last Leaves

Illusions fall away from us like husks
          To leave the fruit – Experience –
Whose flavour may be often bitter, yet
          Invigorating nonetheless…
          Rousseau thought Nature was the balm
          And consolation for all pain.
And sometimes I seek out a favourite grove
At Clarens, lost in mist, just north of Paris –

But all that now is changed. Ermenonville!
          Where ancient idylls still were read –
No longer will I see your twofold light
          Like Aldebaran's elusive star
          Now blue like dusk, now tinged with rose…
          Or Adrienne and Sylvie – twin
Aspects and facets of a single love,
One, its ideal; one, sweet reality.

Where are those shaded groves and lakes: Othys,
        Montagny, Loisy, Chaâlis…all
Discarded sieves from which the past has drained.
        Sometimes I need to see again
        These scenes of reverie. I find
        Sad traces of that distant time
When affection raised the natural
Into art; I savour all that's lost –

And so I smile at lines of Roucher cut
        Into a rock and once admired,
Or maxims carved above a grotto pool
        Sacred to Pan…The ponds, dug out
        At great expense are stagnant now,
        Disdained by swans… The Condé hunt
No longer rides by here with answering horns…
The road to Ermenonville is overgrown.

In Dammartin I sometimes spend a night
        At the *Image of Saint John*, an inn
Where there is still a pier-glass in my room,
        And tapestries adorn the wall,
        And bric-a-brac is undisturbed.
        I sleep beneath an eiderdown
And in the morning, from the window, gaze
On green expanses, stretching miles and miles.

The poplars look like soldiers massed in ranks
        And here and there are village spires.
I could see Ermenonville but for the fact
        That this philosopher's retreat
        Neglected steeples… In such calm,
        I set out for the confectioner's shop
And greet its owner. 'Hello, Curly-head!'
He shouts, 'Hello, little Parisian!'

We spar a moment, then I run upstairs
        To shouts of children's startlement
And Sylvie's smile. I say to myself: this is
        True happiness. And yet…

While Curly-head insists on making lunch,
        We take the children for a walk
Through the avenue of limes, past the remains
        Of the old brick château towers;

And while the children play, we sit and read –
        A little poetry, perhaps,
Or a page or two from one of those short books
        Which are so rare these days.

I forgot to say that, when Aurelia played
        At Dammartin, I took Sylvie
And asked her if she thought Aurelia
        Resembled someone we both knew.
        'Whom do you mean?' 'Why, Adrienne!'
        She laughed aloud, 'What an idea!'
Then sighed and said, 'Poor Adrienne. She died
In the convent here, in 1832.'

The Fifth of October

From the final pages of *The Count of Monte Cristo* by Alexandre Dumas

'... No, I am calm,' declared Morrel and gave the count his hand.
'My pulse is normal. But I feel that I have reached the goal
Beyond which there is nothing more. You asked me to delay;
I've done as you required and suffered for a further month,
In which time I have waited, hoped, God only knows for what,
Since Valentine no longer floods the world with radiance.
You named the fifth day of October. It is now three hours
Away. Release me, Count. You, whom I would have called a god –
Were you not mortal – you must conduct me to the gates of death.'

> And Monte Cristo said, 'Let it be so:
> Come.' And Morrel who let himself be led,
> Was dazzled by a brilliant light.

A brilliant light, a blaze of perfumes, cloud-like carpets; here he met
An air replete with possibility like spilling sherbet foam.

Morrel stepped back. The count said gently, 'Do not hesitate.
Why should these last three hours of life not pass in luxury,
As Romans soon to die, condemned by Nero, spent this time
At tables piled with flowers breathing death in generous gusts
Of heliotropes and roses?' Maximilian smiled. 'Why not
Indeed, if death is merely death and brings to us its prize,
The loss of grief? But let us speak as men.' 'Proceed!'
'Count!' said Morrel, 'You are the font of knowledge and appear
To have descended from a world far wiser than our own...'

'There is some truth in this,' replied the count.
And smiled, 'in that I have descended from
The misty planet we call Grief.'

'I venture then to ask you, Count, as one who almost seems to be
Death's confidant – must Death be met accompanied by his sister, Pain?'

Their dining table, set with candelabra, glowed beneath
Huge statues bearing on their heads rich cornucopia;
The count looked at Morrel with indescribable tenderness,
And said, 'Doubtless, release of soul by force of will may well
Be painful if it is achieved with violence. If you plunge
A dagger into flesh, or trust the bullet's wayward path,
Then certainly you will suffer.' Morrel said, 'Yes, I understand
That Death, like life, must have its secret pleasures and its pain.'
The count sighed. 'Death is either a friend who rocks us as a nurse,

Or enemy who drags us from ourselves.
Some day when mankind learns to live in calm
This may be otherwise; perhaps,

Then, Death will be as sweet and as voluptuous as slumber in
The arms of your beloved. This ideal may well be some years off…'

'And if you wished to die, Count, would you know the secret of
Such ease?' 'Yes, Maximilian, I do.' 'Then I understand
Why you have brought me to this fragrant, luminous cavern. Here
You have prepared for me one of those fragrant, luminous deaths
Which you describe…a death which will allow me to pronounce,
And hear myself pronouncing, Valentine's name, and see her face
Departing and arriving in a single moment's calm.'
'Yes, you have guessed it,' said the count. 'That is what I intend.'
'I thank you,' said Morrel. 'The idea of such death is sweet.
But I entreat you, Count, do not prolong
My suffering.' Monte Cristo said, 'You know
        I have no living relative
And think of you as if you were my son, whom to protect, I would
Forfeit my life – or fortune which amounts to a hundred million francs –

That you might live.' Morrel said coldly, 'Count, I have your word.
The time is drawing close to midnight.' Candelabra flared.
The count said, with a smile, 'Well then, I see you are resolved.
Prepare yourself.' He crossed the chamber and unlocked a chest
With panels chased and carved and graced by sinuous Caryatides,
Four angels reaching heavenwards, out of whose hands he drew
A golden casket opened by a hidden spring. A phial
Contained an unctuous and elusive substance whorled like oil
With many colours. Then the count produced a gilded spoon

  And, pouring into it some nacreous drops,
  Said gravely, 'This is what you asked of me'
    And gazed steadfastly at Morrell.

'I thank you from my heart,' the young man said. 'Adieu,
my generous friend.
I go to Valentine to tell her everything you've done for me…'

And slowly, without hesitation, Maximilian
Consumed the clouding liquid. Both were silent. By degrees
The lamps grew fainter in the marble hands which held them high;
The fragrances grew fainter; objects in the room appeared
To toss like vessels in a storm at sea, then lose their form…
He did not know this death was resurrection without death,
That this strange elixir was much akin to that with which
The count had saved the life of Valentine, had interposed
This soporific for the poison meant for her, and then
  Had overseen her funeral ceremonies,
   And afterwards had brought her body here,
    Patiently to be revived…

An overpowering sadness took possession of Morrel; his hands
Relaxed their grasp; he tried to speak to thank the count
for this calm death.
Then it appeared to him that Monte Cristo smiled, and smiled
Not knowingly, but with the kindness which a father shows

An infant child. A torpor infiltrated all his veins
And flooded into every last capillary. Ideas
Like new forms in a kaleidoscope came floating into view.
He wished again to thank the count and press his hand. His eyes
Closed languidly, but through their prison lashes he could see
A form he knew. It was the count, who opened wide a door
Upon a brilliant light in some adjoining palace room:

> A woman of the most sublime, surpassing
> Beauty stood outlined in light, then crossed
> The threshold of the sun-filled room.

He knew this woman. She was Valentine. Therefore he must have died,
And be in some immediate company of angels. 'Valentine!

Valentine!' Morrel cried from some distant valley, where his soul
Spoke, but no sound could pass his lips. And Valentine approached.
He sighed and closed his eyes. The count called gently, 'Valentine,
He calls you, he whom death would here have taken. Happily
I vanquished death in both of you. Henceforth you shall remain
Inseparable, since he embraced death to discover you…'
She seized the count's hand with an irresistible impulse
Of joy, and brought it to her lips. The count at long last felt
The lowering of this weight into the scale to counterbalance

>   All the evil he had known and wrought.
>   An hour passed before the pulse of life
>   Returned to Maximilian,

Watched tenderly by Valentine. He stirred. He found himself alive
And, for a moment, blamed the count – then saw the face of Valentine.

La Forza del Destino

From Chapter 6 of *Hidden Faces* by Salvador Dali

Reaching the hotel lobby, Grandsailles noted he would be
Too early for his sombre meeting with Veronica.
The gathering storm increased his thirst;
Entering the bar, he told himself, 'I'll have one glass
Of ice-cold mineral water' – for he had resolved
To drink no alcohol. The bar was empty. Dominique
Who knew him well, proposed, 'An armagnac?'
'Yes,' said the Count, yielding at once. 'It will restore
My scattered spirits. How this prospect crushes me!'
The generous glass was filled beyond its line;
Grandsailles lifted his hand to counteract
The prickling in his cheek. The storm approached.

The private mansion of Veronica Stevens aped the style
Of New York's oldest houses, yet
Seemed oddly like the others in the street.
The taxi trip had chilled the Count. The biting cold
Had numbed his skin and made him think his face
Was covered by its tracery of scars. He rang the bell.
The English servant, ushering him in, was elegant,
And the Count of Grandsailles took delight in taking off his gloves
With lingering ease, appreciated here at least.
Next, he was led through faintly glowing rooms,
As if the moon suffused an ocean pool,
And then along a gallery which led at last
To the drawing-room where Veronica Stevens stood,
Her back turned, dressed in white, surrounded by
Three Afghans lying at her feet.

Rock-crystal candelabra swathed in voile
Were ranged along the corridor which seemed interminable;
The light was similarly faint and submarine.
Grandsailles leaned heavily on his cane;
Veronica was watching him approach
In the mirror hung above the fireplace.

As he advanced, the Count of Grandsailles felt the heavy fire
Of armagnac which poured into his veins
The molten lead of all his native Spain. The electric air
Made his rheumatic body heavy. And the storm
Was still impending. Veronica did not move.
He held the cross of pearls and diamonds tightly in his hand.
He felt alarmed, uncertain how to break his dreadful news:
Randolph had died – he whom Veronica loved
But never saw; the Count had been entrusted to return
This cross to her… He felt strangely alarmed.
Veronica had not moved, yet, watching his reflection, seemed
To recognise him when she turned –
Despite the fact that they had never met.
She hastened to him. Drawing close,
She seemed to know all he was struggling to announce.
He was about to speak. Veronica, without a word
Cast like a stone between them, seized his clenched hand.
He still said nothing, thinking now no word could be
As eloquent as opening his fingers. This he did.
Veronica seized the cross and fell in tears into his arms.

He pressed her to him with that suave,
Enveloping symmetry which seemed derived
From trees made elegant by topiary
In old French gardens. He stood still,
Arboreal and protective. She seemed like a tower
In such a grove, surrounded by this canopy.
He waited for her grief to ebb, while holding her;
His eyes, distraught, made moist by tenderness,
Surveyed, through the pale, dense curtain of her hair,
The rich ensemble of the drawing room.

Outside, the day had darkened. Snow began to fall.
Inside, the two black marble fireplaces glowed,
Facing each other with symmetrical fires.
Above them, parallel opposing mirrors relayed
Each other's images until their infinity –
In which Veronica still wept in Grandsailles' arms –
Was lost in greenish haze. The three Afghans
Like pacing buttresses gave their support.
Just at that moment – when the snow began
To settle into steady and determined fall –
An unforeseen thing happened. Veronica
Was not now weeping, and had lifted her bowed head
And, with her eyes half closed, she brought her face
Close to the Count's, offering him her lips.

At once he understood what could not be undone
By any words of his now vastly late… He murmured,
'It's impossible!' and as he spoke –
Regretting that he had allowed the cross
To break its own news so ambiguously –
He raised a hand to touch a painful scar
Causing his cane to fall and roll across the floor.
This clumsiness exacerbated all his wounded pride,
His pain compounded with the affront
Of identity mistaken and now carried past
Disintrication. She, meanwhile,
Observed his slightest movements, thinking she understood
His hesitation, seeing which
She loved him all the more. She spoke
In a voice that might have seemed the voice of rage
Had it not been the more imperative of passion:
'If you had not come back, I should have died
Of that accumulating malady of loss
Which tortured me relentlessly. How can you be afraid
That scars or any other injury could intervene

Between us, when I loved you – even though
Your face was masked in its enveloping hood
Because of frightful injury… To love without the loved one's face!
You cannot think how greatly I have suffered.
I even seemed to have no memory of your gaze
And – like a woman blinded – did not know
That it was you I watched reflected in the glass

Until I held the cross which I had given you.'
She raised it to her lips, then, suddenly,
Began to pace the room in an extreme
Of agitation watched with gravity
By the three reclining Afghans: Grandsailles thought
She seemed to be avoiding certain intricacies
Of pattern in the rose and lotus blossom rug…
She looked at him and said, 'Forgive this nervousness.
It's happiness that makes me weep like this.
It's nothing; it will pass.'
'Alas,' said Grandsailles, 'I am yet to tell you everything –'
'No! No!' Veronica cried, through welling tears,
'I love you, only you, no matter what I hear.'

The Count of Grandsailles found himself still hesitant,
As if this had become his only state…
Veronica's body in his arms was warm. She breathed. It seemed
The world of all delight had been compressed
Into this form, increasingly desirable…
They stood together thus, by fate united, made one by
The double-headed serpent, Chance,
Whose fierce determination cannot be undone…
Veronica's fresh tears were sweeter now. The Count
Remained still culpably, irreparably silent
And each new second of misunderstanding sealed
More absolutely their entwining lives.

In his imperialistic gaze, each thing he saw,
Each porcelain or crystal object, every strand
And tangle of Veronica's hair began
To glisten with the iridescent and malefic fire
Of opals. Even the snow, now falling heavily,
Seemed conspiratorial. In every object which proclaimed
Its independence and identity, he saw
The glitter of his own concupiscence. Each left
Its searing mark. Yet, like a coward, Grandsailles asked himself,
'How could I dare to tell this woman who
Has even now regained her happiness, that the man
She is convinced I am is dead, and that I am
An emissary of his death?' Veronica was
Supremely beautiful – and even if she had not been,
Would not the fever of her ardour have sufficed
To overwhelm him with desire?… Confusion reigns
And pleasure is its grateful subject. With his loss of self
And her new memories of him faceless, false–
He would become another! So resolved,
He took her face between his hands and kissed her mouth,
And so confirmed this future floating without anchor,
This charitable and traitorous lie by which
They set in place their future life.

A letter from Pierre Girardin, notary:

> My dear Monsieur Grandsailles,
> You read this while the danger to our ancient plain
> Is at its worst in the relentless, reckless hands
> Of mining and the disastrous industries of war;
> The vineyards of Saint Julien have been ravaged, all
> Becoming inaccessible terrain behind
> Barbed wire and power cables. Even – dare I say –
> Even the Moulin des Sources is threatened. Were it not
>
> For the efforts of Madame Solange de Cleda, who
> Keeps your best interests uppermost in mind and heart,
> These ravages would be complete. She often asks,
> 'What would the Count have wished in such and such a case?'
>
> Immediately following the ball you gave,
> Madame de Cleda came, offering to save,
> With unrelenting zeal, the Moulin des Sources.
> At once she ordered that the devastated plain
> Be planted for a second time with cork oaks – all
> In weather favourable to them, rain dispersed
> By spells of humid sun… For seven months they've grown
> And, in new leaf, assume the stature of small trees
> Which soon will yield fresh cork. They stand like rows of men…

> Dear Count, I do not wish to seem presumptuous
> In speculating on relations as they stand
> Unhappily between you and Madame Solange.
> My conscience would disturb me nonetheless, were I
> Remiss in noting her condition: she is pale;
> She suffers your severity and your neglect;
> She never speaks of it, but I am peasant enough
> To recognise those curling leaves which indicate
> The ailing tree which withers slowly from within.
> Madame de Cleda has that true nobility
> Which suffers silently. I beg you to think of her.
> And now I ask you to accept, illustrious Count,
> The unconditional devotion of your humble servant,
>
>   Pierre Girardin.

At once, Grandsailles replied by writing to Solange de Cleda.

> Ma chère Solange,
> No man was ever bowed by destiny
> More cruelly than I in writing this,
> To tell you – at the very moment fate
> Has married me to Veronica Stevens – that
> I love you, and that this enveloping love
> Is no mere divagation of the brain
> But that of passionate husband for a wife.

Alas, this mask of incongruity
Is no delirium. I have in vain
Tried to awaken from this nightmare – yet
This marriage is as inescapable
And inescapably real as is my love
For you. Incredible as this may seem,
The circumstances by which mindless Chance
Has tangled all my actions in its net
Would beggar all belief… And yet I must
Insist that I esteem Veronica
And in her happiness must lie the means
By which I must redeem my double wrong,
Against her, and another who has died
And who has placed his trust in me. But now,
Dear, beautiful, beloved Solange (to use
Such terms as I may never use again)
While I begin to know the unhappiness
Which you have known, and your contempt
May let you quite forget me, I shall not
Be able to forget you. You have become
My conscience. One thing only must remain
My consolation: to confess this love
Is punishment for all my former pride.

I greet you with unlimited respect,
And thank you for the oaks which you have planted.
                    Hervé de Grandsailles.

Lighea

From the story by Guiseppe Tomasi di Lampedusa

The senator's apartment was surprisingly well kept;
Heaped books extended from the entrance hall
Through several rooms, and reached at last the senator himself

In dressing gown of camel-hair – or rather, llama wool –
A gift, I learned, of Lima Academic Senate.
He pointedly did not get up, yet greeted me cordially.

He poured some resinated Cypriot wine – a gift, once more,
This time from the Italian School in Athens –
And, offering me Torinese cakes, he almost smiled

And, in a way, apologised for previous attacks
On what he thought my dissolute affairs.
'I know, my friend, I have been quite excessive in my terms,

But, please believe me, moderate in my concepts.' As he spoke,
He fed a large black dog. 'This creature, Corbera,
Is more like the Immortals than your sullen mistresses and whores.'

I did not see his library. 'To one like you,' he said,
'Failed morally in Greek, such classics could
Have no great interest.' But his study where we sat disclosed

Few books – the plays of Molina, Lamotte Fouqué's *L'Undine*,
And, based on it, *Ondine* by Giraudoux,
Then, strangely, much of H.G. Wells (for which he voiced contempt).

But all the walls were hung with splendid, life-sized photographs
Of Greek archaic statuary:
The *Rider* in the Louvre, the *Seated Goddess* from Berlin,

The *Phoebus* at Olympia, the famous *Charioteer,*
The *Korè* of the Acropolis,
The Delphi *Warrior*. The room seemed flooded by their smiles,

Ecstatic yet ironic, glowing with their arrogance.
'You see, dear Corbera,' said the senator,
'These gods shout "Yes!" Your seedy mistresses and whores bleat "No".'

And on the mantelshelf were ancient amphorae and urns:
Odysseus tied to the mast…
The Sirens cast from some high precipice at his escape…

'All petty bourgeois nonsense, that, dear Corbera. No one can
Escape the Sirens, no one. And, if they could,
Those goddesses would never be sufficiently concerned

To kill themselves like that – that is, of course, if they could die…'
I noticed then another photograph,
Faded, framed modestly, which showed an almost naked youth

With long, unruly curls, and features of unusual grace.
Perplexed, I paused thinking I'd understood,
But no. He said, 'And this, my fellow countryman, this was

And is, and shall be still, Rosario La Ciura.' So!
The senator in dressing gown had been
A young, resplendent god. But then we spoke of other things.

He said, 'I am to speak at a conference in Portugal;
I sail in May from Genoa on the *Rex*
With French and German conference members. Like Odysseus

I'll stop my ears so as not to hear their nonsense. But there will
Be, nonetheless, some lovely days on deck,
Long days of sun and blue and salt smell of the confiding sea.'

Soon after this I left, and felt this visit had ensured
That our relations were now cordial.
I took the trouble to obtain for him some excellent

Sea urchins; these with Etna wine and peasant bread
Were waiting for him when, quite timidly,
I asked him to my humble rooms. He came, and passing through

My bedroom, laughed. 'So. Here we see the theatre of your poor
Plebeian rutting. And what books are these?
Quite good. Perhaps you're less plebeian intellectually

Than I'd allowed. This Shakespeare was not quite devoid of worth:
"sea change into something rich and strange.
What potions have I drunk of Siren's tears." The man at least

Knew something.' Later, when we sat to lunch and I produced
The Genoese sea urchins on a tray,
He was in ecstasies. 'You thought of this! How can you know

That these are what I yearn for most? I thank you, Corbera.'
I said, 'You're safe in eating them. They're fresh –'
He laughed. 'You people fear decay, and strain your ears always

To the shuffling steps of Death. A pity that they aren't still wrapped
In seaweed from the Augustan coast – these spikes
Have clearly never made divine blood flow…' But as he ate,

Absorbed and lacking gaiety, he likened once again
Their strange, partitioned, blood-red flesh
(As he had done when, in that sombre café, we first met)

To the female – puzzling, tasting of the sea, sea plants and salt.
He sighed and sipped some wine. I noticed then
Two tears which surreptitiously he wiped away. He spoke

Of Sicily – despite an absence of some fifty years,
Returning only briefly to discuss
At Syracuse some abstruse aspects of Greek Tragedy.

'But tell me again about our island, always beautiful,
If inhabited by donkeys…' I recalled for him
The waving corn seen from the windy heights of Etna in May,

The scent of hillside rosemary, the taste of honeycomb,
The solitude near Syracuse, the gusts
From orange groves near Palermo – which, some say, only come

At sunsets at the end of June. Enchanted nights
At Castellamare bay, when anyone
Who lies back under the stars may lose his spirit into them…

He talked about the sea, and seemed to have remembered all
Its dark intensities which are
Essentially Sicilian. 'And have you ever been

To Augusta, my good Corbera?' And, when I said I had,
He asked, 'And did you ever see that inner part,
That little tidal bay past Punto Izzo, where the hill

Looks down on salt pans?' 'Yes, indeed,' I said, 'It is
The loveliest spot in all of Sicily and, so far,
Unspoilt by any of our swarming Fascist Leagues of Youth.

A wild place, isn't it? Deserted, not a house in sight;
The sea is peacock-coloured; opposite,
Beyond the iridescent waves is Etna. Nowhere is

So masterful, so calm, so silent, so divine.' He smiled,
Was silent, then said, 'You're a good lad, Corbera…
Now fetch that little car of yours, if you please, and take me home.'

We met again as usual in the weeks that followed. We read
Sicilian news sheets in the sombre bar;
The senator seemed still inclined to talk of Sicily.

And now we took nocturnal walks along the Via Po
And through the bleak Piazza Vittorio
To watch the rushing river and the hill where spring would soon

Be prodigal. The lilacs had begun to flower; and here
Young couples braved the damp of winter grass.
'In Sicily the sun already burns, the fish appear

On moonlit nights in phosphorescent spray. Yet here we stand
At this insipid and deserted stream, and hear
The moans of these brief couplings like the sighs of approaching death.'

But he was greatly cheered by thoughts of his departure. Soon
He'd be approaching Lisbon by the sea.
He took my arm. 'You should accompany me – a pity, though,

There's no provision there for people lacking Greek – and if
Zuckmayer thought you weren't proficient in
The optatives of the irregular verbs, you might be asked to leave.'

Two days before he went, he asked me to his house to dine:
Again the picture of the gods, again
The faded photograph of one who, once a youthful god,

Now seemed dismayed by his own metamorphosis; white-haired,
Slumped in a chair, he seemed intent on speaking:
'Now, Corbera, if I've brought you here tonight and put at risk

Your fornications at the Rivoli, it is because
I need you. At my age, when one sets out,
There are no certainties, the more so if one trusts the sea…

And, since I really am quite fond of you, I should at least
Explain the reason for my oddities
And much that I have said, which must have made you think me mad.

I wish to tell you something which I rarely speak about,
Something which happened when I was that man –'
He pointed to the photograph. 'A long time ago,

Or so it must appear to you, in 1887,
When I was twenty-four, and looked like that,
I was a Classics graduate and had already earned

A certain reputation for some modest studies on
Ionian dialects. I was preparing to compete
For a chair at Pavia University. To say the truth,

I have to tell you this – that never before that year, or since,
Had I, or have I, known a woman. There!'
I thought my face had stayed marmoreally impassive, but

I was deceived. 'That wink of yours is ill-conceived, my friend.
I tell the truth, and also boast. I know
That we Catanian males are generally thought capable

Of impregnating even our wet nurse. But not for me:
To spend one's days and nights with gods and demigods,
One can resist the brothel stairs at San Birillio.

Religious scruples also held me back, in those laced days…
But, Corbera, your eyelashes again
Betray you! My little Corbera, you can scarcely have

A notion of the endless labours needed to compete
For such a chair in Ancient Greek.
The language, luckily, I knew as well as I do now;

But, for the rest – I do not wish to boast – the variants,
Both Alexandrian and Byzantine,
The innumerable connections linking literature and myth,

Philosophy, philology and science! I repeat,
It's quite enough to drive a person mad.
And so I lived on little more than coffee and black olives

While studying, and cramming wayward boys for their exams
To pay my keep. And then came that appalling summer.
At night the sun was vomited again in Etna's flames;

The heat by day was suffocating; metal railings burnt
The unwary hand; the lava paving stones
Seemed on the point of melting. Every day the sirocco flapped

Its slimy bat's wing in one's face. I was exhausted. Then
A friend who met me, wandering in the street
Reciting Greek I understood no longer, rescued me:

"Rosario," he said, "I have a rustic three-roomed hut
At Augusta, far from town beside the sea.
I'm off to Switzerland. Pack your bags and go there. Go at once."

He drew a map; I did not hesitate, and left that night,
And in the morning woke to face the sea
With Etna in the background much subdued in morning mists.

The house contained a couch on which I spent the night, three chairs,
A table; stoneware pots, a lamp; outside,
A fig tree and a well. I saw no one. Then, in the town,

I made arrangements with the peasant mentioned by my friend
To bring me pasta, bread and vegetables
From time to time. I hired a tiny fishing boat and, with it,

Lobster pots and fishing lines. At once I was resolved
To stay at least two months. The heat! The heat
Was still intense but, rather than reverberate from walls,

It seemed to generate a brutal, fluid energy;
And in that heat the sea seemed to recede
And leave a multitude of diamonds on its surfaces.

My studies ceased to be an effort. Books became, instead,
Not obstacles, but keys opening the world,
Whose most entrancing aspects now seemed spread before my eyes.

Thus everything within their pages seemed to float as well
Before me. Often I declaimed the names
Of those forgotten gods, so long ignored, but who appeared

To skim transparently above the sea. This solitude
Was now complete, and broken only by
The peasant's visits. Seeing my exalted, carefree state,

He'd leave provisions and depart, presuming me quite mad.
The sun, and solitary nights beneath
Rotating stars, the silence, meagre food, difficult texts –

All these conspired to predispose a mood for prodigy.
This was fulfilled one day soon after dawn.
I had awoken and at once rowed out some way from shore,

Then sought the shadow of an overhanging rock; the sun
Already climbed in ferment, pouring gold
Across that watered silk, the azure, unresisting sea.

I was declaiming ancient verses on this tide of blue,
When suddenly I felt the boat edge sway
As if behind me someone were about to climb on board.

I turned and saw her rising from the sea, a smooth-faced girl
Of sixteen, two small hands upon the gunwale;
She smiled. Her pale lips showed a glimpse of little, sharp, white teeth,

Sharp like a dog's. But it was not the smile that people give
Debased by pity, cruelty
Or irony… This smile expressed itself alone – that is,

An almost animal delight, divine exultance, joy
In being all she was… This guileless smile
Was the first of many spells she cast; while from sun-coloured hair

Seawater flowed down over green, wide-open, childlike eyes…
Our captious reason rankles at such sights,
And tries to harness memories of the obvious: I thought

I'd met a girl out bathing. Holding out my hands I leaned
To help her in. But she, with vigorous ease,
Emerged straight from the sea as far as her waist and put her arms

Around my neck, enclosing me in some marine perfume
Which I had never known, and slipped into the boat.
Below her groin her body was the body of a fish,

Covered in minute scales of glittering blue and mother-of-pearl,
And ending in a supple tail, which beat
Idly against the bottom of the boat. She was a Siren.

She lay back with her head supported on crossed hands, and showed,
With serene immodesty, the delicate down
Of armpits, firm breasts tightly drawn apart, and perfect loins.

Again I noted what at first I'd thought a scent, but which
Was more some magical essence of the sea
– Or else it was the breath of youthful sensuality…

We were in floating shade but, twenty yards away, the beach
Seemed utterly abandoned to the sun.
And, being almost nude, I could not easily conceal

The effects on me of all this dazzlement. And then she spoke.
Her voice was even more remarkable
Than was her smile and smell of sea foam. I was overwhelmed,

Submerged in this slightly guttural, reverberating voice.
Behind the words one sensed the lazing surf
Of summer seas, the winds of lunar waves… And then I knew:

The music of the Sirens, Corbera, is no more than this,
Their speaking voice. She spoke in Greek and yet
I found it strangely difficult to understand. She said,

"I heard you talking to yourself in words I understood.
I like you. Take me. I am named Lighea,
Daughter of Calliope. Do not believe the tales

Invented of us. We kill none of you. We only love."
Bent over her, I rowed as if into
Her laughing eyes. We reached the shore. I took that shimmering body

In my arms, and passed from solar glare into the shade.
She was already bringing to my mouth
The flavour of such pleasure as became inestimable,

And which, compared to your avowed carnalities, would seem
Like wine compared to water from the tap.'
He spoke with certainty, as if this were the recent past;

Never for a moment did I think the senator
Was telling lies. For there was nothing here
Which did not seem to have the truth of sun and sunlit sea…

And equally I felt that my own sexual vanity
Had been exposed, reduced to trivialities
By the penetrating light of this remembered blue and pearl…

'So those three weeks began. It is not proper, nor would it
Be kind to you, to enter into details –
Suffice to say that these embraces, frequent and intense,

United those extremes of pleasure, namely, the spiritual
And elemental… Think of what Balzac
Dared not express explicitly in his 'A Desert Passion'…

For those immortal limbs relayed such life-force that, always,
Each loss of energy was soon restored –
I loved as much as all your Don Juans in their entire lives.

And oh, what love! Immune from convents, crimes, commander's rages,
Leporellos' trivialities,
Pretensions of the heart, sham deliquescence, false sighs…

(A Leporello did in fact disturb our passion once:
I heard the peasant's heavy step outside,
And drew a sheet in haste across Lighea's shining tail.

He saw her head and arms and, thinking this some village girl
He signalled with increased respect, and winked
And made a gesture of male solidarity, then left.)

Sometimes she'd disappear for several hours, and then return
More ardent, and I'd hear that voice again
Like lapping water on a sloping shore with tiny waves.

In fact, she often plunged into the sea and went away,
And then would meet me in the boat, or else,
If I were still indoors, would slither over pebbles, half

In the water and half out of it, and call to me for help
To climb the slope. Her lower body then,
So agile in the sea, took on the vulnerability

Of wounded animals, an aspect cancelled by her smile…
She ate from the sea, and only what was alive;
Sometimes she would emerge, her slender torso glistening,

And in her teeth a shining fish still quivering, with its blood
Staining her mouth and then – when cast aside –
The sea. And then her voice, Corbera! Her voice was like the call

Of conch-shell trumpets echoing over ruffled seas. When, once,
I gave her wine, she was incapable
Of drinking from the glass but gulped it from her open hands

As dogs drink with their tongues. Her eyes would widen with surprise
At such an unfamiliar flavour. Afterwards
She did not ask for it again. At times, she'd come ashore

With molluscs which I opened with a knife for her... Dear Corbera!
As I have said, she was both beast and yet
An Immortal, and it is regrettable that speech cannot

Continually express this synthesis with just that grace
Which she conveyed by her own flesh and blood,
A grace which was accompanied and augmented by her voice.

Not only did she show great joyousness and delicacy
Encountering the carnal act (so free
From dreary animal lust) but in her speaking voice I heard

Intense particularity which I have found elsewhere
In only one or two great poets. Not for nothing
Is she the daughter of Calliope. Ignorant

Of culture and official wisdom – and contemptuous
Of moral inhibitions – she belonged
To the fountainhead of culture, wisdom, immortality...

Sometimes she spoke of Pan and self-renewal. Then she'd say
"While you are young and handsome, follow me.
My dwelling place is under mountainous dark water. Come.

Remember I have loved you and, when you are tired and cannot
Go on, lean on the sea and call me. I
Will always answer, since I am everywhere, and can assuage

Your thirst for sleep." She told me of the sea depths, bearded Tritons,
Bright translucent caverns. These, she said,
Were unreal visions. Under them the truth lay deeper, deep

In bland, mute palaces of formless waters… I could not
Distinguish all these mysteries from the voice
Which told them so mysteriously… And then, one day, she said,

"I must go far away. I know a place where I can find
A gift for you." When she returned, she held
A branch of lilac coral, shell-encrusted, luminous…

For years I used to keep this in a drawer, and kiss
The places I remembered the Indifferent –
That is, the Beneficent One – had touched it. Later on, a maid

Could not resist its novelty and gave it to her ponce.
I found it later on the Ponte Vecchio,
Cleaned and polished, desecrated, drained of all its life,

And bought it back and that night sadly cast it to the depths
Of the Arno… Sometimes too she spoke
Of other human lovers she had taken during her

Millennial adolescence – fishermen and sailors, Greek,
Sicilian, Arab and Capresi… Some
Were shipwrecked mariners, adrift on rotting rafts; to them

She appeared a moment in the tempest's lightning flash, to change
Their lingering death to ecstasy. "And all of these
Have summoned me again in time, as I would have you do."

Those weeks of summer passed as quickly as a single day,
But, afterwards, I realised that I had lived
For centuries. That young, lascivious girl, that cruel wild beast,

Had also been a Mother of all Wisdom, who had razed
All faiths, unsettled metaphysics…and
Who had led me with her fragile, often bloodstained fingers to

A true repose, eternal, knowing and beneficent.
She also formed in me an asceticism
Denied, not from renunciation, or the sullen will,

But from an incapacity to savour once again
Inferior pleasures. Certainly I shall
Not disobey her call, could not refuse to speak aloud

To the sea when it is time… Perhaps due to its violence,
That summer ended quickly, late in August.
The first drops fell, tepid as blood. The nights were a chain of slow,

Mute lightning flashes, seeming on the horizon like
The cogitations of a god. At dawn
The sea, dove-coloured, would exclaim and moan like turtle doves,

Arcane and restless, and in the evening crease like drying cloth
Without the slightest sign of breeze – smoke-grey,
Pearl-grey, steel-grey, divided and striated like the clouds.

Mist grazed the water; maybe, on the coast of Greece, the rain
Had come already. And Lighea's mood
Changed like the sea from dawn to dusk. She fell more often silent,

Spent hours stretched on a rock and seldom went away. She said,
"I want to stay with you. If I leave now,
My sea companions will not want me to come back again.

There! Do you hear them calling me?" Sometimes I thought
I heard a long sustained and lower note
Amidst the screech of the seagulls. "They are blowing on their shells

And summoning Lighea for the festival of storm."
And that broke on the 26th, at dawn.
The sea was twisted in confusion. Wind-waves formed. We smelt

The scent of rosemary bushes. Then the wave broke on our rock.
The Siren cried, "Goodbye. You won't forget!"
And disappeared into the iridescent sprays of surf.'

The senator left next morning. At the station he seemed still
As grumpy and acidic as before,
But, as the train began to move, his fingers reached out from

The carriage window, and just grazed my head. Next day there came
A telegraphed report from Genoa:
During the night-watch Senator La Ciura had been lost –

Had fallen from the *Rex* as it was steaming on to Naples,
And, although lifeboats were launched at once,
The body of this celebrated scholar was not found.

After a week his will was read; the money in the bank,
Together with his furniture, was left
To his recent maid; the library of several thousand books

Was given to the University of Catania;
And, by a recent codicil,
I was bequeathed the Greek vase with the Siren figures, and

The splendid photograph of the *Korè* from the Acropolis.
Both objects I sent home to Palermo.
Then came the war, and I was stationed at Marmarica,

Rationed to half a litre of water a day. And there I heard
That 'Liberators' had destroyed my home.
On my return, I found the photograph cut into strips

To serve as torches for the looters. The large bowl was smashed;
The largest fragment shows Ulysses' feet
Tied to the mast against a glimpse of sea. I keep it still.

The books were stored in cellars at the University,
But, as there is no money for more shelves,
The Collection *Rosario La Ciura* slowly rots away.

www.ingramcontent.com/pod-product-compliance
Lightning Source LLC
Chambersburg PA
CBHW062143100526
44589CB00014B/1675